Blank Arcade 2015
Games out of Joint

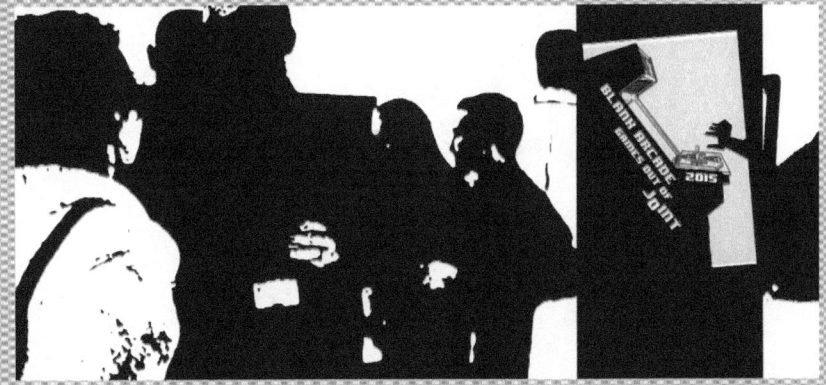

Copyright © 2015

Event curated by

Lindsay D. Grace
http://www.LGrace.com

and

Paolo Ruffino
http://paoloruffino.com/

First Printing: May 1, 2015

ISBN 978-1-329-10309-2
Lüneburg Germany

More information about the event can be viewed at

http://BlankArcade.CriticalGameplay.com

Artworks

- A Tactile Physical Rehabilitation Game
  Niels Quinten
- Arthur Rimbaud in Liberty City
  Colleen Flaherty and Matteo Bittanti (Coll.eo)
- Bottle Rockets
  James Earl Cox III
- Colorigins: A Tactile Color Mixing and Matching
  Game, Brad Tober
- CONTROL - an experimental (meta) game about
  interface constraints, Kieran Nolan
- I Wish I had the Boy
  Eliran Vegh
- polyCopRiotNode_
  Adam Trowbridge & Jessica Westbrook (Channel Two)
- Sibi
- Roberto Fassone
- Stealth
  Martin Reiche
- Zelda Deforested
  Mark Franz

Digital Games

- **404Sight**, 404 Sight Team (University of Utah)
- Skyward Level 404, Singapore University of
  Technology & Design (SUTD) Game Lab
- Splattershmup Team Splattershmup (including Andy
  Phelps, Aaron Cloutier, Christopher Cascioli and
  Jenn Hinton)

Artist Workshop Selections:

- Nothing Remains Unseen, Perola Bonfanti
- Lindsay Grace, Black Like Me

Overview

Blank Arcade: Games out of Joint is more than just a sequel, mod or expansion pack. It revisits its own concept through an exhibition of experimental games and artworks that push the boundaries of game design and theory. The curators invited artists, scholars and designers to propose works that investigate and question the 'instrumentality' of entertainment.

We are more and more surrounded by video games that propose to be more than just 'for fun': games for health, education, social and civic engagement and so on. But what else can games be? How can games be used for trouble-making, rather than problem-solving? How can games become environments for posing new questions about our society, beliefs, and lives in general?

The exhibit balances physical play with digital play, and its intermediaries. It also seeks to embrace the complex relationship between creative and empirical research. The selected works demonstrate varied creative efforts to fill in the blanks of ludic experience, offering new game play experiences, highlighting spaces that are relatively uninhabited by other playfulness.

This is an international collection, with participating artists from North America, Europe and Asia.

Curated by Lindsay D. Grace and Paolo Ruffino

Shapes:
A Tactile Physical Rehabilitation Game.
Niels Quinten

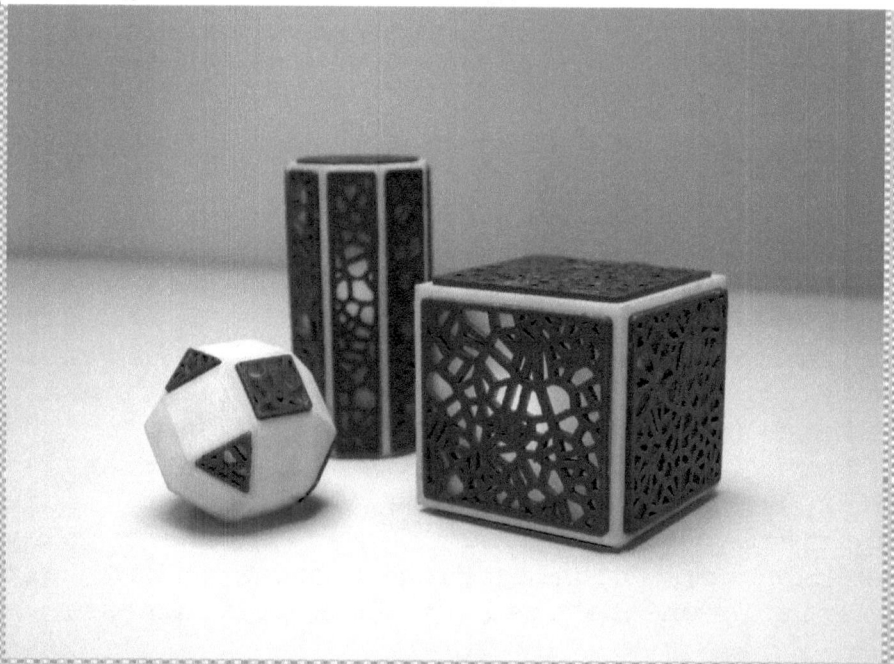

Shapes

The game Shapes consists of a collection of physical interactive objects with simple geometrical forms. The outline of these objects is shaped by polygons or plane surfaces. A number of these polygons on each object provide interactive input and output capabilities. For example, these polygons light up either when players touch them or when two or more objects touch one another. As each of these interactive polygons have their own sensor and light, a wide range of light-configurations can be achieved on a single object, and even more when multiple objects are combined. The overall goal of the game is to combine these individual objects in a wide variety of arrangements. This is done by performing basic physical actions such as lifting, rotating, dragging or pushing these objects in order to bring them together. Whenever a different combination is formed, the color and brightness of the interactive polygons is altered, and thereby new courses of action are suggested. There is not one specific goal or set of rules for the game. Rather, the objects can be arranged according to different sets of rules.

Shapes is one of the results of an artistic research project on the design of physical rehabilitation games, with a focus on neurorehabilitation (e.g. stroke survivors). The objective of the project was to explore how a game design style could be developed in order to support the specific requirements of a particular rehabilitation therapy (i.e. incorporating upper-limb physical exercises, adjusting the game to the diverse abilities of patients, etc.) as well as the abilities of the patients (i.e. dealing with cognitive impairments such as low vision, memory problems, etc.). By using artistic methods such as abstraction and minimalism, we aimed to create a game style that is created out of the rehabilitation context, rather than lending game forms directly from entertainment games. In this sense, the resulting game Shapes is interesting because it provides a novel perspective to rehabilitation game research by raising questions: how do we want rehabilitation games to look and feel? Do they need conventional display screens? Do they need a separation between the real world and the virtual world? Do they need elaborate, figurative game worlds?

Arthur Rimbaud in Liberty City
Colleen Flaherty and Matteo Bittanti (COLL.EO)

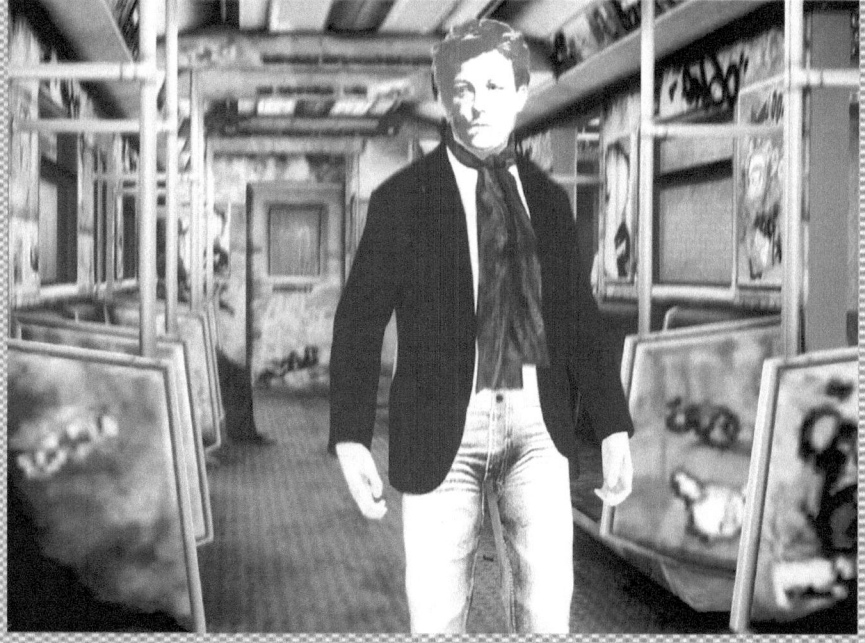

Arthur Rimbaud in Liberty City

Arthur Rimbaud in Liberty City is a replay of David Wojnarowicz'(1954-1992) photographic series Arthur Rimbaud in New York (1978-1979) developed within the virtual spaces of Grand Theft Auto IV (Rockstar Games, 2008). Created by COLL.EO in collaboration with Iranian modder Amir Goreyshi, Arthur Rimbaud in Liberty City consists of 48 black-and-white images projected as 35mm slides and a set of framed photographs. The third in a series of interventions in Grand Theft Auto IV, Rimbaud in Liberty City challenges already fragile notions of the "authentic self", updating a previous performance in RL that prefigured the fluid role-playing of the digital age. This project brings issues of authorship, identity, and representation into the Game Art sphere.

Arthur Rimbaud in New York is considered David Wojnarowicz' first significant body of work. It consists of twenty-five black-and-white photographs of a young man, posing as Wojnarowicz himself, wearing a mask with a reproduction of a portrait that Étienne Carjat had taken in 1871 of Arthur Rimbaud. Each of the photoshoots took place in various settings of New York City, both private and public, between 1978 and 1979. Wojnarowicz saw in Arthur Rimbaud a model, an alter ego, and his idealized self. He developed the project with a borrowed camera, using three different friends as models.

COLL.EO's Arthur Rimbaud in Liberty City is both a homage and an appropriation. To be precise, it is an appropriation of an appropriation , since Wojnarowicz's project was inspired by the work of Ernest Pignon-Ernest, a Fluxus and Situationist French artist, whom he discovered while visiting Paris in 1978-1979.
Arthur Rimbaud in Liberty City examines the status of masculinity within a virtual world marked by explicit chauvinism, misogyny, and homophobia. Moreover, by reproducing and wearing Rimbaud's paper mask that Wojnarowicz produced by photocopying the photograph of Carjat's portrait within the spaces of Liberty City and posing in similar settings, COLL.EO not only decontextualized the artist's "original" gesture, but also reframed it. Rimbaud's trajectory through visual culture can therefore be considered as an exercise in media archeology. As such, the modded GTA IV becomes a playful archive, a repository of art interventions, intermissions, and intrusions.

Projected onto a screen by a mechanical slide projector, each image of Arthur Rimbaud in Liberty City poses questions concerning the value and meaning of ludic performativity, that is, the role-play activity that takes place in the so-called "magic circle". Taken in places familiar to most players of Grand Theft Auto, COLL.EO's screengrabs are an example of post-photographic practices in the age of videogames.
Finally, Arthur Rimbaud in Liberty City may suggest that ludic spaces are an alternative to the increasingly gentrified urban environments of New York and San Francisco, where artists, teachers, low-income workers and middle-class families - the new pariah - have been ruthlessly erased from the public sphere by the ruling class of brahmins. Arthur Rimbaud in Liberty City alludes to urban, political, and social life under the regime of Neoliberalism. Virtual reality is the only alternative to the winners-take-all politics of real estate.

Bottle Rockets
James Earl Cox III

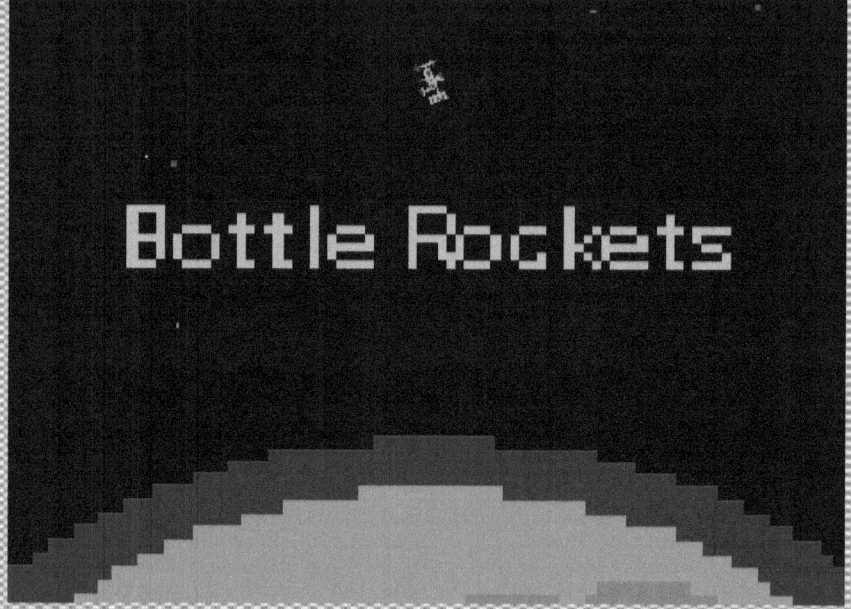

Bottle Rockets

Bottle Rockets is a music video(game) about a mother and her daughter inspired by and made to Aphex Twin's song Alberto Balsalm. As such, rather than take the spotlight for itself, the game was created to add emotion and meaning to its featured track. This is accomplished by a set of constraints: the game must be inspired by the song, the game must conclude when the song does, the song must be the only audio within the game, and the game cannot interrupt the song.

Colorigins:
A Tactile Color Mixing and Matching Game
Brad Tober

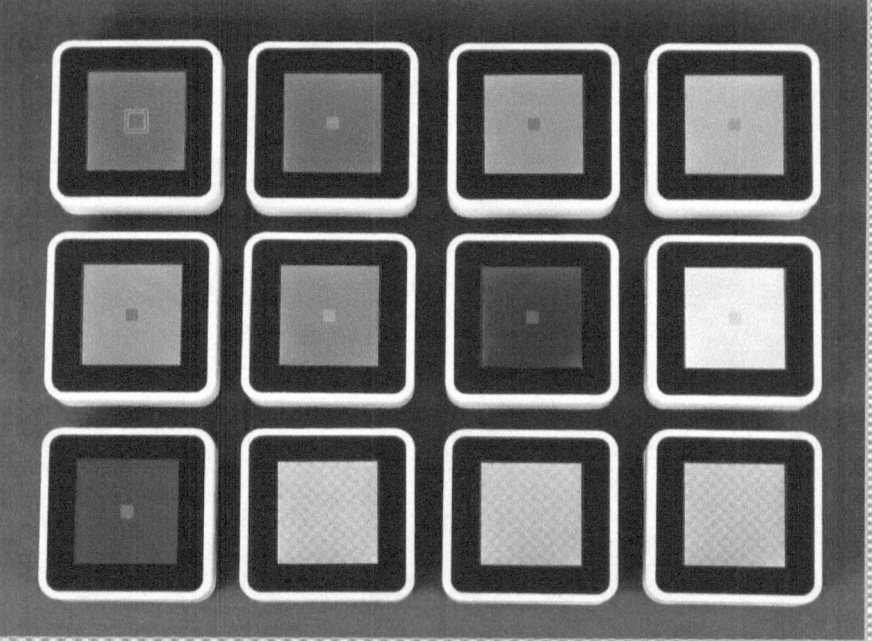

Colorigins

Colorigins is a tactile color mixing and matching game designed and developed for the Sifteo Cubes tangible computing platform. Colorigins presents a softly gamified approach to learning elements of subtractive color theory. The game objective is to accurately match a randomly generated target color by mixing it from a set of source (conventional primary and secondary) colors. Throughout the process of color mixing, players can gain experience with concepts such as value, saturation, tints, shades, tones, complements, chromatic neutrals, and the relative visual strengths of particular colors. Mastering the use of color is critical for both artists and designers because it is one of the most powerful tools these practitioners have to use in communicating a message or idea. Given two works that are otherwise formally identical, a single difference in color can have a profound effect on how the work is interpreted or understood.

The affordances of a manipulative, or learning tool, like Colorigins rely heavily on both the physicality of the experience it offers and how this physicality informs the interface presented to a user. In the case of Colorigins, the aesthetic simplicity of the Sifteo platform hardware—consisting of up to twelve 1.7-inch square cubes that connect wirelessly to a base station that stores and runs software developed for the platform—is balanced by its relatively complex technical capabilities. The cubes each feature a touch sensitive LCD, an accelerometer, and proximity sensors so that the cubes know when and where they are in contact with one another. Fully leveraging these features enables the design of a user interface that is both minimal and intuitive. For Colorigins, this fuses the distinctively physical experience of mixing color (like paint on a palette) with the advantages of the digital medium (such as the custom color mixing algorithm implemented by Colorigins).

Control-an experimental (meta) game about interface constraints

Kieran Nolan

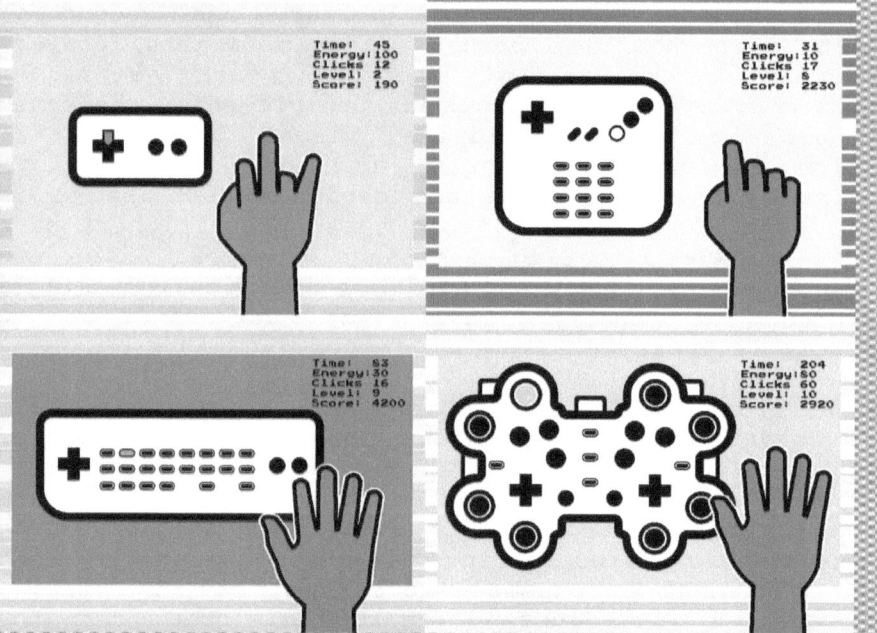

Control

CONTROL is an art game experience that intends to provoke discussion and reflection on the limitations of the physical interface and the nature of the human computer symbiosis in videogaming as mediated through the manual game controller.

The game takes place in a computer that is part early IBM PC compatible, part tape loading 8bit home micro. Use the basic arcade control scheme of 8 directions and one action button to control a downsampled representation of your hand, while negotiating a series of increasingly complex videogame control devices.

CONTROL has 10 levels. The first 9 of these are based on existing videogame controllers, while Level 10 is the 'OctoPad', an experimental concept prototype. The player must successfully press all the highlighted controls to proceed to the next stage. If the timer or energy level reaches zero then it's 'Game Over'!

I Wish I had the Boy
Eliran Vegh

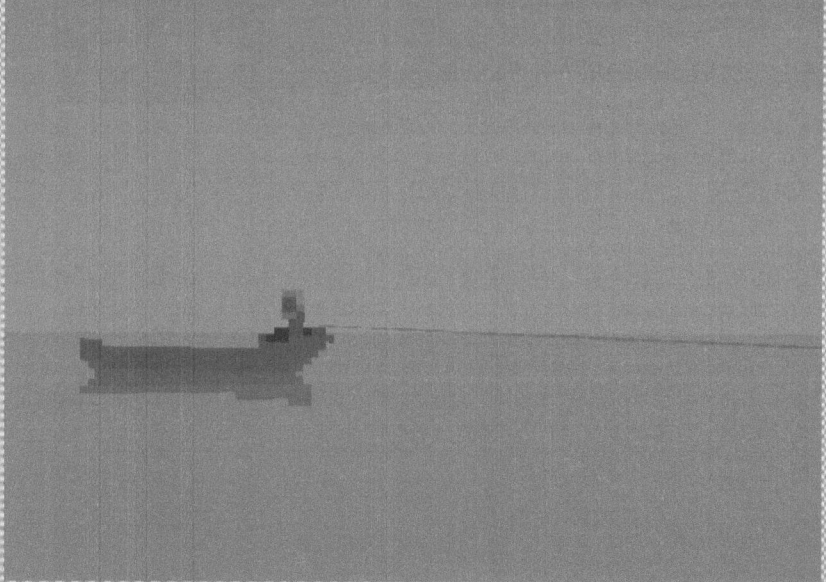

I Wish I had the Boy

"I wish I had the boy" is game that was inspired by the book Old man and the sea by Ernest Hemingway, in the game the player has to hold the right arrow on the keyboard along with the space bar for 3 days to help the old man Santiago catch the Blue Marlin, if the player will not hold the keyboard keys the fishing line will slowly leave the screen and the game will restart, However every 6 to 8 of hours the fish starts to struggle and the player will have to vigorously tap on the left arrow, right arrow and spacebar for a couple of minutes until the fish gets tired or the player gets tired and
loses the fishing line line. The game's visual representation is very minimalistic, most of the game all that the player will see is a the old man leaning on his back and the fishing line leading to out of the screen, accompanied by quite sea and clear blue skies. To indicate that the time is moving forward in the game, the background changes slowly from day tonight.

In I Wish I Had the Boy the artist forces the player to sit and stare at the image of the old man and sea for 3 days, staring at the sky change from day to night, how the old man's boat rocks gently onto the water while slowly watching the fishing line getting closer. In this game the player will have to find a way to occupy himself for the 3 days journey while forced to interact with the keyboard to operate the game. Its personal physical and mental endurance, that happens outside the game's fictional world.

polyCopRiotNode_
Adam Trowbridge and Jessica Westbrook

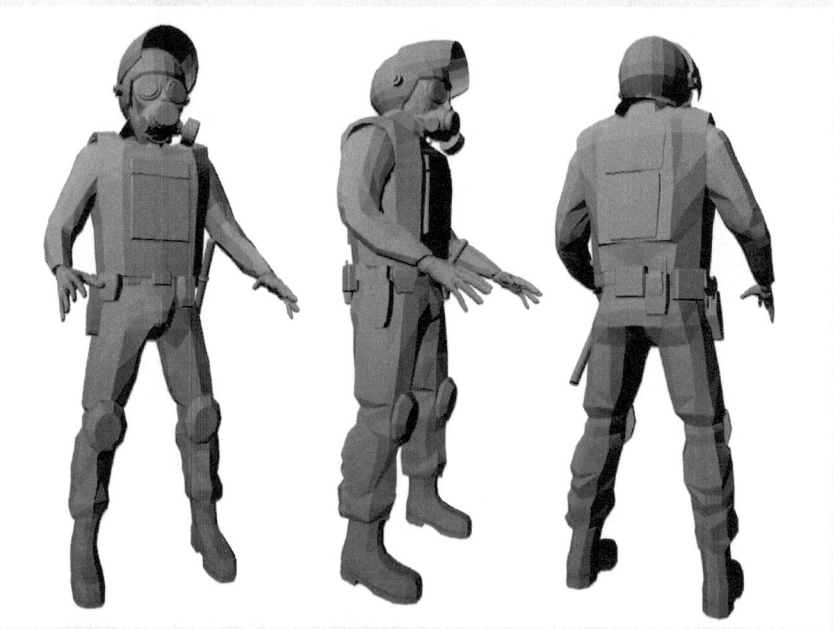

polyCopRiotNode_

polyCopRiotNode_ is a site-specific augmented reality (AR) public artwork system accessed via a free downloadable Android or iOS app. Each PolyCopRiotNode_ location is surrounded by 2 story tall riot police making visible what is ordinarily invisible: increasingly hostile suspension of community, and arrest of non-commercial uses of space/time.

Currently polyCopRiotNodes are found in Chicago, IL, Cleveland, OH, Portland, OR, New York, NY, and Washington, DC. In each implementation of the project, a network of polyCop augments are situated/revealed in specific geolocations based on our research of local police incidents and activity. For example: polyCopRiotNode_DC counter-narrates incidents where DC police have used excessive force on unarmed civilians in the privacy of their homes, based on a narrative derived from the police departments own erroneous information. In recognition of recent events in NYC, PolyCopRiotNode_NYC places nodes on every corner of the street of NYC. This results in an omnipresent police presence and, at the same time, highlights the immense size and power of the NYPD, which former-Mayor Michael Bloomberg called his "own private army."

PolyCopRiotNode_ came about through a learned understanding that activity outside the priorities and value systems of capitalism, whether intervention, occupation, or cultural production generally involves an overreaching, and increasingly militarized response by police. The name of this work, polyCopRiotNode_ suggests that it is a network of instances, of a class of power paradigms and ideologies.

Sibi
Roberto Fassone

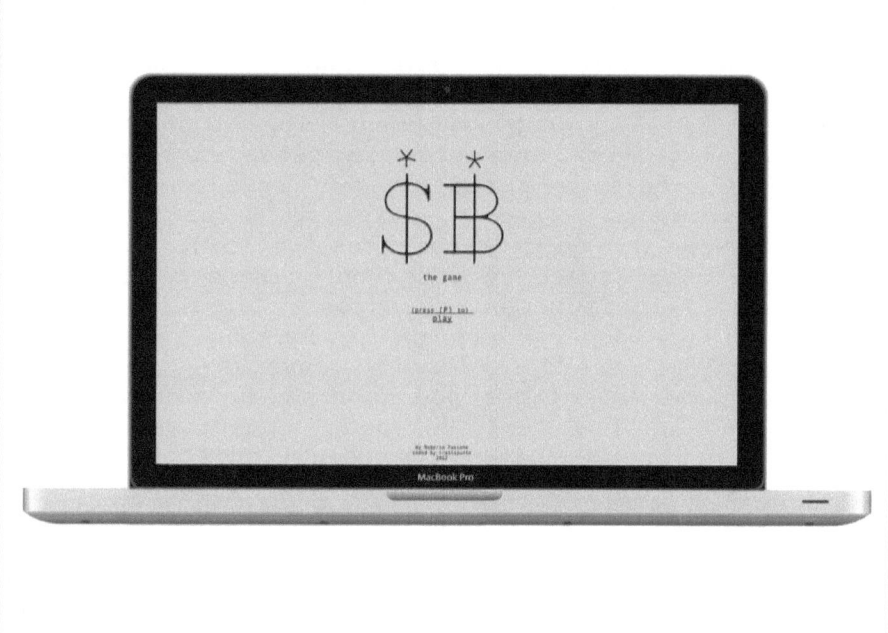

Sibi

Sibi is a software able to generate more than 50 billions of sets of instructions useful to produce potential artworks.

Every set consists of six boundaries: three are connected to the medium (M), two are connected to the aboutness (A) and one to the title (A) that the player is asked to make.

Sibi is a project that deals with the concepts of art, creativity and game.

Sibi is online and available for free at play.sibisibi.com.

Stealth
Martin Reiche

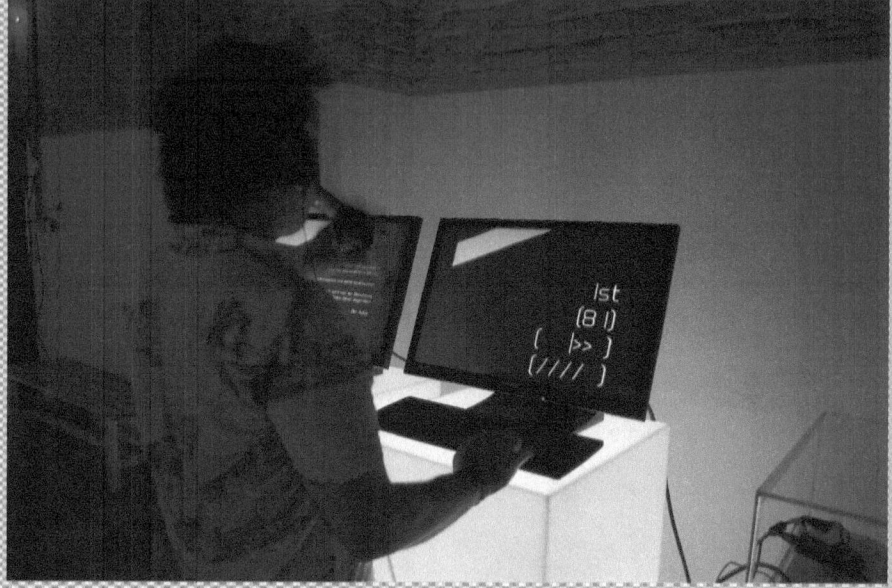

Stealth

Stealth is an auditive racing game that shows how the "easy" task of listening can be hard and complex if you as a player are not used to trust your ears but your eyes. The player slips into the role of the blind driver of a high speed car in a two-dimensional world. He has no other choice as to find his way based on what he hears. Leaving the track and crashing with objects will result in acoustic punishment and the player will eventually realize that the whole game is not really about driving a car through an acoustic labyrinth, but about how we perceive our very world.

Stealth takes the player into a world of music and sound, addresses the representation of reality in the gaming environment and aims to re-contextualize it through a simple and intuitive game design.
The player's patience and adaptability are stressed and a new understanding of what a game can be is established.

Zelda Deforested
Mark Franz

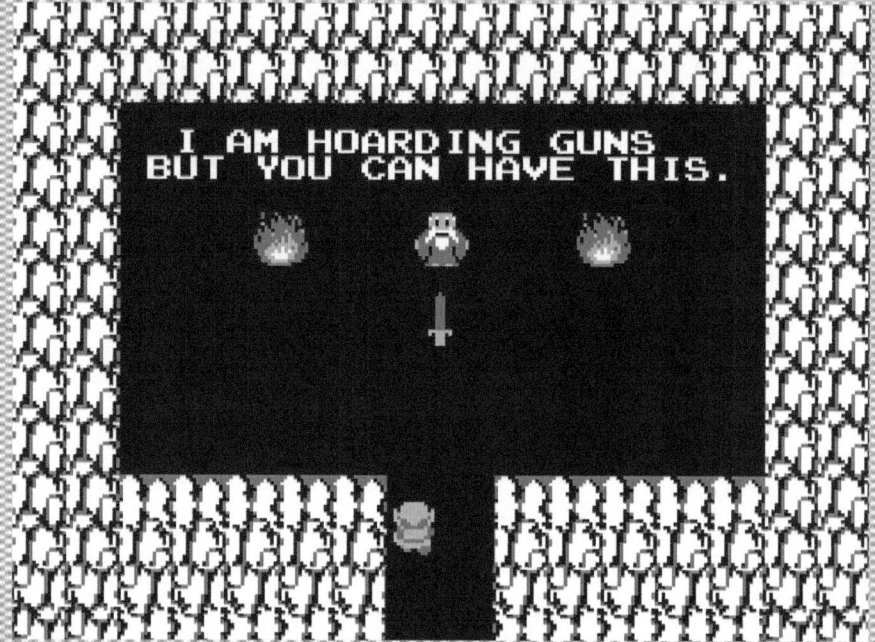

Zelda Deforested

Zelda Deforested is a serious game that revises the Legend of Zelda by removing all of the forest elements and replacing them with a rocky and monotone landscape. The graphics and sound have been recoded to create a new narrative in which the protagonist is found in a dystopian world where people have taken to living underground due to changes in the environment. Within these bunkers the protagonist encounters characters hoarding supplies and trying to deal with the struggles of living life underground. Only one animal species has survived in a terrain without trees and water. The hero has
taken to hunting in order to gather food and barter for tools.

This work was created by altering the hexadecimal code found in the original Nintendo Entertainment System game, Legend of Zelda. The characters and maps from
the original game have been manipulated and recoded to provide a new narrative. The interactive nature of this piece is important for bringing visitors into a dialogue about what has changed in this game. Although many players will be familiar with the original Zelda video game, this reconstruction intends to challenge others to critically consider what has also changed socially, culturally, and technologically since the game was created in the 1980's.
Additionally important is that this interactive work questions whether an art piece using technology can elicit a response that is anti-technology. In other words, whether technology can be a medium for self-critique is considered in Zelda Deforested.

Ultimately, users are encouraged to reflect on the various roles of technology in modern life and how technology relates to the natural world. How humans engage each other and their natural environment and whether they can work collectively toward social, economic, and environmental sustainability are additional questions posed by Zelda Deforested.

404Sight
404 Sight Team

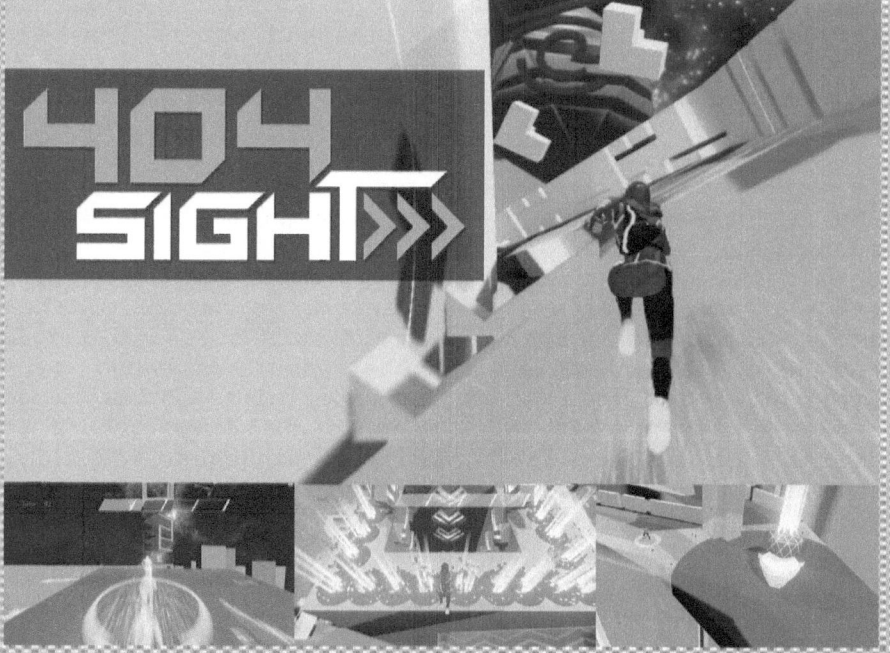

404Sight

404Sight is a free game made in support of net neutrality. It's a 3D playground runner influenced by the parkour running style of Mirror's Edge with the addition of a special ping ability that reveals areas that can speed the player up or slow them down. Hidden fast and slow lanes become visible and it takes a bit of planning to plot a course through a world full of hazards – especially when the internet service providers themselves are actively trying to impede the player's progress. In 404sight, the player attempts to traverse a level as quickly as possible without getting throttled by the ISPs, who actively throws slow tiles and inhibitors in their way.

Skyward
Level 404
Singapore University of Technology & Design (SUTD) Game Lab

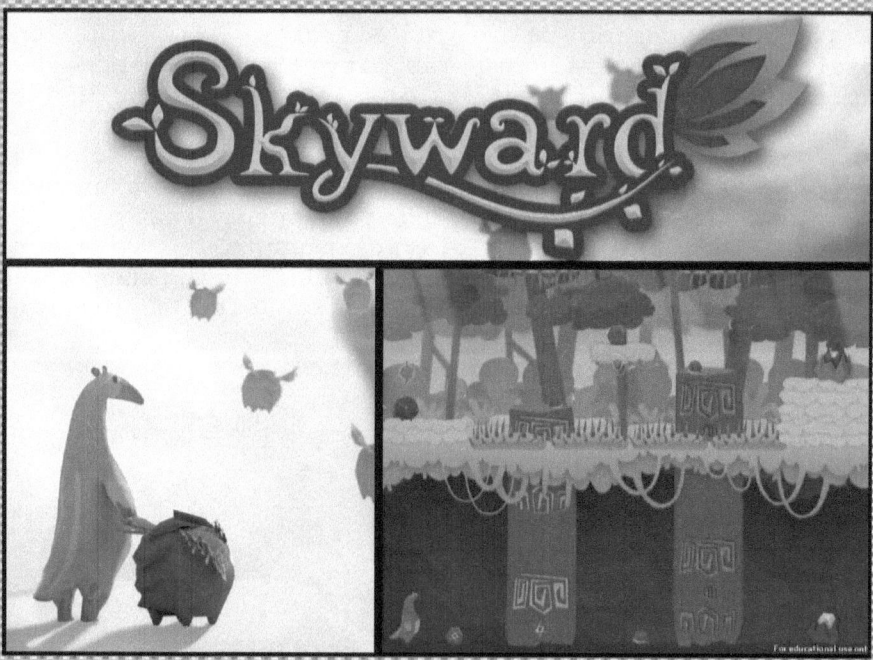

Skyward

Skyward is a 2D puzzle platformer which integrates the changes in character mechanics with cooperation between two characters to foster empathy for the disabled. In this game, two mystical characters set forth on an exciting journey in a fantasy world. These characters possess unique abilities and are determined to support each other in getting through the dangerous forest populated with natural traps and deadly creatures.
In collaboration with SG Enable, an agency dedicated to enabling persons with disabilities, our goal was to develop a game to encourage empathy for persons with disabilities. We aimed to empower persons with disability, appreciating our differences and thus create awareness in our community that disability does not equate to incapability.

The style of the game has gone through its own history of changes. In the prototype stage, the two main characters cooperated by performing actions simultaneously and at times combined into one character. The idea then evolved into three characters working together, with only one character in the game at a time. After rigorous play testing and feedback, we eventually settled on the current mode of having two characters co-existing but never physically meeting on the same plane, yet helping each other by affecting their surroundings using their abilities.

Through a series of logical reasoning puzzles and timed sequences, you will maneuver two characters with distinct abilities to reach their final destination, to be reunited with their families. A creature of the surface and a subterranean dweller will for the first time overcome obstacles in their paths – but only with your assistance! In order to clear a level, you must carefully move both characters as loss of either life will prevent you from moving forward. Reliance of one character on the other is key to meeting the challenges. This links back to our design philosophy of engaging players in an awareness and appreciation of our differences, and how despite certain limitations, we can overcome them with a bit of help.

Splattershmup
Team Splattershmup

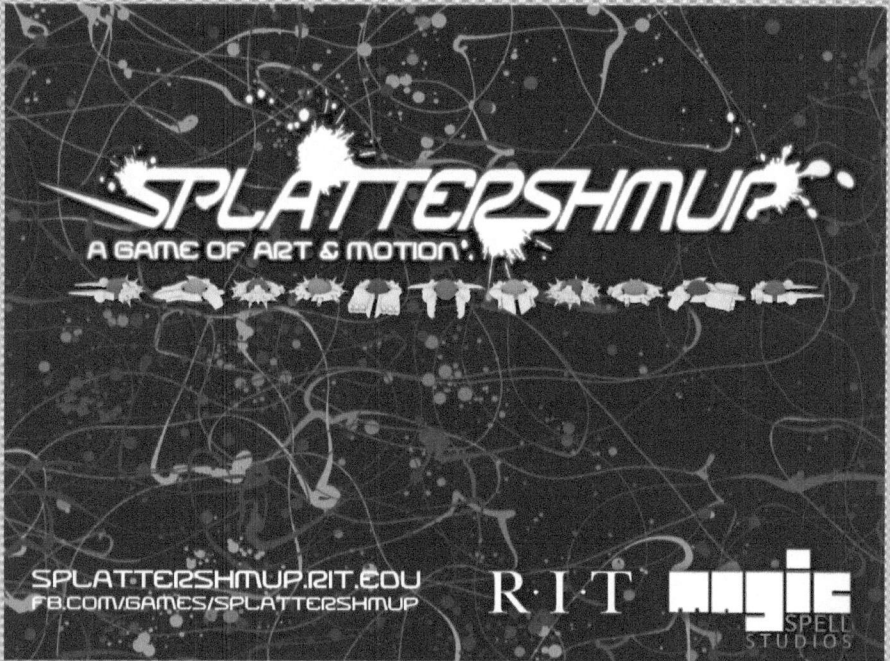

Splattershmup

Splattershmup is a game that explores the intersection of the classic shoot-em-up (or "shmup") arcade game and gesturalized abstration or "action painting" (a term coined by critic Harold Rosenburg in 1952 and often used to describe the work of American artist Jackson Pollock). It is intended to allow the player to reflect on their in-game actions and strategy through visual record, and to approach the creation of art as an arena of action. Art can thus be created, shared and discussed that comes "from inside the moment" of game-based decision. Splattershmup was produced in residence at the Rochester Institute of Technology in a studio course offered by Professor Andrew Phelps and Mr. Aaron Cloutier through the School of Interactive Games and Media, with guidance and development support from the RIT Center for Media, Arts, Games, Interaction & Creativity (MAGIC).

It is published and maintained through MAGIC Spell Studios, LLC., and can be downloaded from http://splattershmup.rit.edu.

Nothing Remains Unseen
Perola Bonfanti

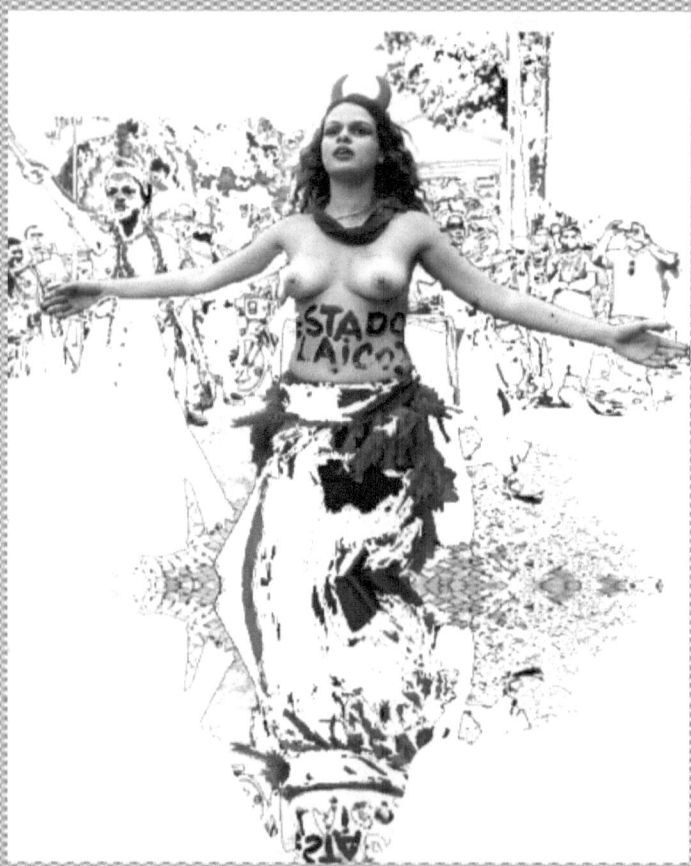

Nothing Remains Unseen

Nothing Remains Unseen is an art game built especially for the digital platform, not only taking it as its media, but also bringing it along with its concept. The poetic of the game relates historical, existentials and contemporaneous subjects in a semiotic platform to enable the player to experiment with new ways of communication at the same time they look inside themselves.

Taking hand of manipulated images from recent riots from Brasil, historical images and quotes, video art riddles, GIFs and animated cliparts, the project invites the players to explore relevant subjects in abstract and concrete forms creating a correlation between the individual and the system.

Starting the game at the art piece the player is directed to a website by scanning a QR Code. The game evolves in a seguênce of pages using buttons, internal and external links.
The objective of this game is to bring to the surface changes that the digital reality is generating in the way we perceive time, reality and freedom. Taking hand of the new medias to propose a different art game platform and enables the player not only to get affected by the poetic, inspired by the ideas, but investigate themselves through the journey.

Black Like Me
Lindsay Grace | Critical Gameplay

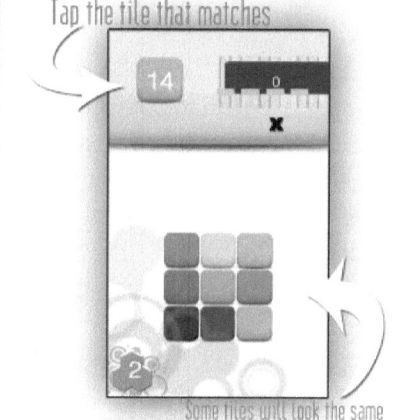
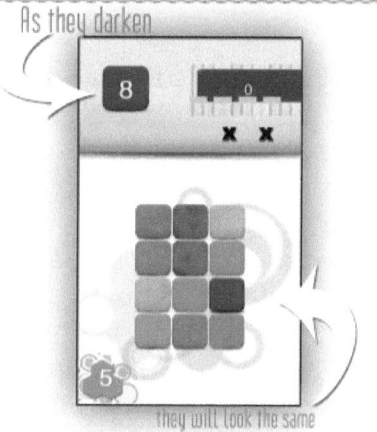

Black Like Me

Black Like Me is ostensibly a simple puzzle game for mobile devices. Players color match the top tile to a tile in the play area to win. The more success a player has, the narrower the color band becomes. What starts as a a diverse color set, soon becomes a series of grays and ends in shades of black. The longer you play, the more the colors look alike.

Ultimately the game is about race and identification. It is procedural color matching. The game employs critical design to encourage players toward situational analysis instead of mere attribute matching.

Players are baited with a color matching game at the surface, but the game is designed to reward players for identifying the behavioral difference between a match tile and all other tiles. Successful players are rewarded for holistically evaluating a scene and subverting the explicitly suggested game rules. The game is designed to train players toward perceiving ambiguity and employing alternative play strategies.

The game is part of the 12 game series known as Critical Gameplay, and available for download at http://www.CriticalGameplay.com

www.ingramcontent.com/pod-product-compliance
Lightning Source LLC
Chambersburg PA
CBHW021851170526
45157CB00006B/2392